HOW TO FIND BIGFOOT

Thomas Kingsley Troupe

BLACK
RABBIT
BOOKS

Hi Jinx is published by Black Rabbit Books
P.O. Box 227, Mankato, Minnesota, 56002.
www.blackrabbitbooks.com
Copyright © 2023 Black Rabbit Books

Marysa Storm, editor; Michael Sellner, designer
and photo researcher

Library of Congress Cataloging-in-Publication Data
Names: Troupe, Thomas Kingsley, author.
Title: How to find bigfoot / by Thomas Kingsley Troupe.
Description: Mankato, Minnesota : Black Rabbit Books, [2023] |
Series: HiJinx. Paranormal field guides | Includes bibliographical references
and index. | Audience: Ages 8-12 | Audience: Grades 4-6 |
Summary: "With fun facts, a colorful design, and critical thinking questions,
How to Find Bigfoot inspires readers to take their love of the paranormal to
the next level all while laughing and learning"- Provided by publisher.
Identifiers: LCCN 2020034517 (print) | LCCN 2020034518 (ebook) |
ISBN 9781623107161 (hardcover) | ISBN 9781644665657 (paperback) |
ISBN 9781623107222 (ebook)
Subjects: LCSH: Sasquatch–Juvenile literature.
Classification: LCC QL89.2.S2 T75 2022 (print) | LCC QL89.2.S2 (ebook) |
DDC 001.944–dc23
LC record available at https://lccn.loc.gov/2020034517
LC ebook record available at https://lccn.loc.gov/2020034518

Image Credits

Dreamstime: Joeybear, 20; Shutterstock: Aleksandr Bryliaev, 14, 17;
Aluna1, 5; Arcady, 12, 19; charless, 13; Christos Georghiou, Cover,
10; DenisKrivoy, 8–9; Den Zorin, 9; flaflam, 18; Galyna G, 3, 4, 7, 8,
9, 12, 16, 17, 18; Gmorv, 15; GraphicsRF.com, 18; Grimgram, 4, 5,
16, 17, 22, 23; HitToon, Cover, 1; jamesjoong, 16–17; Lightspring,
12–13; Malika Keehl, Cover, 1, 21; Memo Angeles, Cover, 3, 5, 6, 10,
10–11, 14, 16, 18, 21; monbibi, 9, 14, 17; MSSA, 6; My Life Graphic,
5, 10, 16–17; Natsmith1, 17; Pasko Maksim, 18, 23, 24; Pitju, 6, 11,
14, 17, 21; Ron Dale, 3, 4, 8, 15, 20; SlipFloat, 7; Top Vector Studio,
11; totallypic, 5, 11, 15; Yurchenko Yulia, Cover, 1, 21

CONTENTS

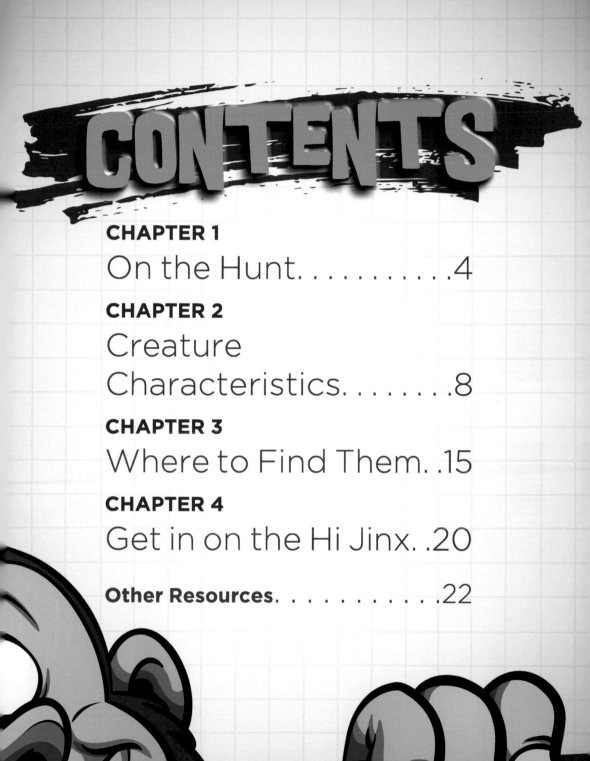

Chapter 1

ON THE HUNT

So, you want to prove Bigfoot creatures exist, do you? Ha! So does everyone else! Finding **proof** isn't easy, though. So far, no one has taken a clear video or photo. And people have been looking since 1958!

If you're still serious about finding one, you've come to the right place. I've spotted a Bigfoot 11 times or so. This field guide will show you how it's done.

Thomas Kingsley Troupe

Thomas Kingsley Troupe is not well-known for his Bigfoot research. But he sure loves talking about the creatures. He claims to have seen a Bigfoot many times. So far, only his mom believes him.

Handy and Helpful

This field guide covers everything Bigfoot. It'll tell you what these creatures look like and eat. It'll even show you where to find them.

So bring this book on your searches. It's like having me in your back pocket, helping you! But please, don't sit on me.

A Bigfoot has many different names. Some people call it "Yowie" or "Sasquatch." In Florida, it's known as the "Skunk Ape."

7

Chapter 2

CREATURE CHARACTERISTICS

To find a Bigfoot, you need to know what they look like. A Bigfoot is about 8 feet (2 meters) tall. Long, shaggy hair covers its body. This hair is often brown, black, or **periwinkle**.* Besides being hairy, a Bigfoot stinks! Do you like how hot garbage smells? Get used to it. That's a Bigfoot's natural **odor**. And they don't like to bathe!

Remember, not everything tall, hairy, and smelly is a Bigfoot. Maybe it's just your older brother who really needs a haircut.

*Expert's Note

OK. No one has ever actually seen a periwinkle Bigfoot. But I'm pretty sure they come in that color.

Behaviors

Not sure if it's a Bigfoot or your older brother? Study how the creature acts. Bigfoot creatures hate having their pictures taken. I've heard them howl to scare **intruders** away. They also like to stomp around and throw boulders.

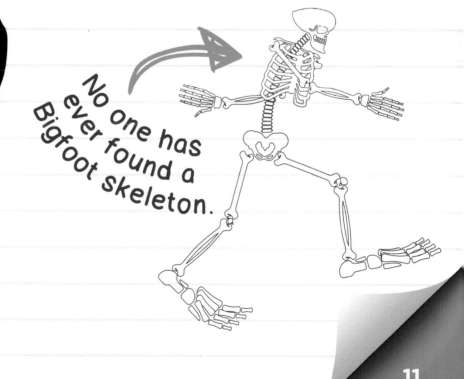

No one has ever found a Bigfoot skeleton.

Diet

Bigfoot creatures aren't allowed in restaurants. Why? Because they don't wear shoes. The creatures must eat what they find in the woods. They often eat fruits and berries.

Some people worry the creatures might get hungry enough to eat children. That won't happen. I believe they just want a bowl of mac 'n' cheese.*

*Expert's Note
If you eat a lot of mac 'n' cheese, be careful. You might smell very tasty.

*Expert's **Note**

Don't make travel plans just yet. I'm just guessing here.

Researchers believe a Bigfoot can run about 30 miles (48 kilometers) per hour.

Chapter 3

WHERE TO FIND THEM

Most experts say Bigfoot creatures only live in forests. A lot of sightings come from the northwestern United States. But I believe that's changed. The creatures are tired of people searching their woods. They've moved. Many of them now live where no one would ever look ... Delaware.*

Delaware

Tracking the Creatures

Looking at the ground is the best way to track a Bigfoot. The creature's big feet will leave HUGE prints. Bigfoot tracks are mostly shaped like human tracks. They're just longer, wider, and deeper.

Not sure it's a Bigfoot track? Get close. Give the print a sniff. It should smell like old cheese and puke.* If it stinks, it's probably from a Bigfoot.

*Expert's **Note** Try not to throw up from the smell. Maybe bring some air freshener with you.

A Bigfoot probably weighs about 1,000 pounds (454 kilograms).

18

Approaching the Creatures

By now, you've probably found a Bigfoot. Of course you did! That's how great this field guide is! Now what should you do? Be nice! Tell the creature how much you like its hair. Maybe give it some black licorice.* Whatever you do, don't take a photo. The monster will hate that and run.

Feel free to thank me for my expert advice. Because of this guide, you now know how to find a Bigfoot!

*Expert's Note

Fruity candy would probably work too.

Chapter 4

GET IN ON THE HI JINX

No one knows if Bigfoot creatures really exist. But you can still search for them. Explore wooded areas with an adult. Visit your library to read books about the creatures. Search the Internet for stories and videos from other Bigfoot hunters! You could be the one who finally proves the creatures are real!

Take It One Step More

1. The world is full of Bigfoot stories. Why do you think people find them so interesting?

2. Why do you think no one has ever found a Bigfoot skeleton?

3. Some people say Bigfoot creatures aren't real. Do you agree with them?

GLOSSARY

claim (KLAYM)—to say something is true when some people might say it's not true

intruder (in-TROOD-uhr)—someone or something that comes or goes into a place where they are not wanted or welcome

odor (OH-der)—a particular smell

periwinkle (PER-i-wing-kuhl)—a light blue color

proof (PROOF)—something which shows that something else is true or correct

LEARN MORE

BOOKS

Owen, Ruth. *Making a Meal for Bigfoot.* Mythical Meals. Minneapolis: Bearport Publishing Company, 2022.

Ransom, Candice. *Legendary Bigfoot.* Spooked! Minneapolis: Lerner Publications, 2021.

Troupe, Thomas Kingsley. *Searching for Bigfoot.* On the Paranormal Hunt. Mankato, MN: Black Rabbit Books, 2021.

WEBSITES

Bigfoot Facts for Kids
kids.kiddle.co/bigfoot

Have You Ever Spotted a Sasquatch?
www.cbc.ca/kidscbc2/the-feed/sasquatch-our-furry-friends

The Evidence for Bigfoot
www.animalplanet.com/tv-shows/finding-bigfoot/lists/bigfoot-evidence/

INDEX